Young Learner's THESAURUS

with Illustrations

Written by
Debbie Fox

Illustrated by
Wladek Szechter

McGraw-Hill Children's Publishing

A thesaurus is a book of words. It helps you to find just the right word for what you want to say.

If you want to find out what a word *means*, you need to use a dictionary. If you want to find *another* word for a word, you need to use a thesaurus.

Why Do I Need a Thesaurus?

Sometimes the same word keeps popping up in your head. You want to tell someone that you have had a good day, but you don't want to use the word "good"! So you turn to your thesaurus, look up the letter "g," and follow the words in alphabetical order until you find the word "good." Some other words you can use instead of "good" will be listed here.

A thesaurus gives you a choice of words that mean the same thing as the word you first thought of. A book like this can help make what you say more interesting or exciting.

For example:

eat
Different ways to **eat**: bite, chew, chomp, munch, nibble, crunch, gobble, swallow

How This Thesaurus Works

In this book there are over 340 main words, or "headwords," listed in alphabetical order. The headword is always shown in heavy **black** type. After the headword is a list of words you can use instead. Then there is an example sentence to show how the word is used.

Sometimes words have more than one meaning; we show you other meanings through different example sentences.

Sometimes we tell you the opposite (antonym) of the headword, and sometimes we give you a list of words that are linked to the headword.

Aa Bb Cc Dd Ee Ff Gg

empty
1. unfilled, not full
   The glass was **empty**.
2. free, vacant, deserted, bare
   The house was **empty**.

Opposite:
full

- headword
- first synonyms
- example sentence
- second synonyms
- example sentence
- opposite (antonym)
- illustration

Where does the word "thesaurus" come from? It comes from the ancient Greek word *thesauros*, meaning "treasure" or "storehouse." We hope you find your *Young Learner's Thesaurus* to be a real treasure chest of new and exciting words to use!

about
roughly, approximately, around, more or less, close to, nearly
He took **about** 20 minutes to get home.
Opposite: exactly

ache

to hurt, feel sore, feel bad, be painful
My finger **aches**.

advice
suggestions, tips, recommendations
Listen to your sister's **advice**.

afraid
to be scared, frightened, terrified, petrified
I'm **afraid** of the dark.

age
1. to grow older, grow weaker, fade
My parents will **age** in the next few years.
2. time, era, period
The **age** of the steam engine has gone.
3. a long time, days, weeks
It took me **ages** to paint this.

alike

identical, similar, the same
The twins dress **alike**.
Opposite: different

almost
nearly, just about, not quite, practically
I'm **almost** there, Luke!

amazing
wonderful, beautiful, magnificent, awesome, fabulous
The setting sun looked **amazing**.

angry

to be annoyed, mad, upset, furious, livid
Jane and her brother were **angry** with one another.

answer
1. a reply, response, an explanation
The teacher waited for an **answer**.
2. solution
There's an **answer** to this problem.

anxious
worried, nervous, tense, upset
Louis felt **anxious** about the test.

argue
1. fight, squabble, disagree
We always **argue**.
2. to say, state, claim, reason
The teachers **argue** that a new gym is too expensive.

attractive
pretty, good-looking, handsome, beautiful
She is an **attractive** woman.

bad

1. naughty, silly, rude, misbehaved
Tom has been a **bad** boy.

2. terrible, horrible, dreadful, awful
I have a **bad** cold.

3. nasty, serious
There was a **bad** accident the other day.

Opposite: good

bag
We will put the apples in a paper **bag**.
Other types of **bags**: backpack, basket, tote **bag**, hand**bag**, duffel **bag**, purse

ball

1. Types of **balls**:
beach **ball**, soccer **ball**, foot**ball**, base**ball**, soft**ball**
Sarah threw the **ball** to her brother.

2. dance, party
Their parents went to the **ball**.

bang

1. crash, explosion, boom, blast, noise
Simon heard a loud **bang**.

2. to hit, bash, bump, knock, whack, hurt, smash
Don't **bang** your head on the door!

bark

to yap, woof, growl, yelp
The dog **barks** when a stranger comes to the door.

beach

1. seaside, coast, shore, seashore
Let's go to the **beach**.

2. sand
We played catch on the **beach**.

beautiful
1. gorgeous, stunning, attractive, lovely
The twins looked **beautiful**.

2. magnificent, breathtaking, glorious, spectacular
The sunset was **beautiful**.

bend

1. to curve, twist, wind
The road **bends** here.

2. to make crooked, curve, shape
Can you **bend** this piece of metal?

3. to crouch, squat, lean
Bend down!

best

1. top, leading, finest, most successful
I'm the **best** runner in my class.

2. correct, right
Is it **best** for me to do it this way?

better

1. easier, simpler
There's a **better** way to do it.

2. well, stronger, fitter, healthier
I feel **better** now.

big

1. enormous, huge, large, tall, massive, gigantic, mighty, colossal
A **big** monster tramped through the forest.

2. important, major, serious
It was a **big** decision for him.

block

1. to obstruct, jam up
The truck was **blocking** the road.

2. lump, chunk, slab, piece
They dropped the **block** of stone.

blow

1. to puff, breathe air into
Blow up the balloon.

2. disappointment, upset, disaster
It was a **blow** to lose the game.

3. The ways the wind can **blow**: gust, howl, blast, puff

boring

dull, tedious, uninteresting, dreary, unexciting
It was such a **boring** book.

bother

1. to annoy, disturb, irritate, bug
The noise outside was starting to **bother** her.

2. to worry, care about, be upset about
It doesn't **bother** me when it rains.

bottom

1. base, foot
Look at the **bottom** of the wall.

2. backside, behind
He fell on his **bottom**.

3. underneath, end
It's at the **bottom** of the pile.

Opposite: top

brave

courageous, fearless, daring, bold, heroic
He was a **brave** warrior.

break

1. to drop, smash, crush, crack, shatter
Make sure you don't **break** it.

2. to fracture
He might **break** his leg.

3. rest, time off
They took a short **break**.

4. to disobey, disregard
Don't **break** the rules!

bright

1. shining, glowing, dazzling, gleaming
The **bright** lights shone.

2. clever, gifted, intelligent, smart
He is a **bright** child.

3. happy, cheerful, glowing
She gave us a **bright** smile.

bring

to carry, fetch, take, get
Could you **bring** the boxes?

bug

1. insect, creepy-crawly
There's a **bug** crawling under my bed.

2. to annoy, irritate, aggravate, get on your nerves
Don't **bug** me!

3. virus, fault, defect, problem
There's a **bug** in the computer program.

4. to put a listening device in, listen in
The police team could **bug** the telephones.

bumpy

uneven, rough, bouncy, jerky
We rode over a **bumpy** road.

burn

1. to be on fire, ablaze
The house started to **burn**.

2. to go red, sting, peel, crack, blister
Don't **burn** yourself on the hot kettle!

burst

1. to break, pop, split
The heavy bag **burst** open.

2. to pop, prick, puncture
He **burst** the balloon.

3. to rush, hurry, charge
Sally **burst** into the room.

busy

1. non-stop, active, hard at work, rushing around
I have been **busy** all day.

2. lively, bustling, hectic, crowded
The city streets are **busy**.

3. in use, engaged, tied up
The phone line is **busy**.

buy

to pay for, get, purchase
I want to **buy** a new bicycle.

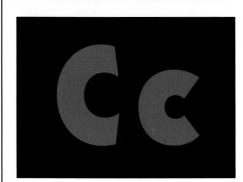

call

1. to cry out, shout, yell, exclaim
I will **call** him over.

2. to name
They will **call** the baby Lucy.

3. to telephone, phone
I couldn't **call** you last night.

4. to stop by, come around, drop in, visit
I'll **call** this morning.

calm

1. flat, smooth, still, peaceful
The sea was **calm**.
Opposite: rough

2. quiet, patient, cool
Keep **calm**, everything is fine!

3. to keep quiet, settle, soothe
The teacher tried to **calm**
the students.

careful

1. cautious, watchful, alert
I'm always **careful** when I walk home.

2. thorough, neat, accurate, organized
He is such a **careful** worker.

catch

1. to grab hold of, hold, seize, grasp
Try to **catch** the ball.

2. to reach, get to, make
I must **catch** the school bus.

3. to pick up, develop, get
I'm sure I will **catch** a cold.

cause

1. to start, create, bring about, produce
They didn't know what **caused** the fire.

2. the reason for, origin, source
He is the **cause** of all our problems.

3. charity, campaign, movement
Help support our **cause**.

change

1. to get dressed, switch clothes
The girls can **change** in the bedroom.

2. to alter, amend, rewrite
I will **change** the end of the story.

3. to become, grow into, develop, turn into
Caterpillars **change** into butterflies.

4. money, coins, small bills
Do you have **change** for a dollar?

chase

to run after, pursue, follow
The dog **chases** the cat.

cheap

1. good value, inexpensive, a bargain
I bought a great coat.
It was **cheap**.

2. nasty, horrid, mean, devious
What a **cheap** trick to play!

3. poorly constructed, poor quality
The **cheap** coat fell apart.

check

to examine, look over, test, inspect
Mom will **check** the brakes on the bicycle for him.

cheerful

happy, bright, friendly, jolly, lively
He was always **cheerful**.
Opposite: miserable

choose

to pick, select, opt for
Which dessert should I **choose**?

clean

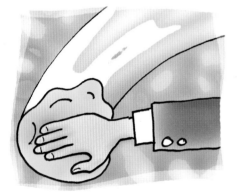

1. to brush, sweep, wash, mop, wipe
Danny will **clean** the window.

2. pure, fresh, unpolluted, clear
The water was so **clean**.

3. spotless, immaculate
Her room was **clean**.

clear

1. cloudless, bright
The sky was **clear**.

2. straightforward, direct, well thought out
His report was very **clear**.

3. clean, tidy, sort out, move, get rid of
I must **clear** this mess.

close

to shut, lock, fasten, bolt
Please **close** the door.

cloudy

1. gray, dreary, overcast, gloomy
What a **cloudy** day!

2. murky, unclear
The water was **cloudy**.

club

organization, society, group
We set up a fitness **club**.

cold

1. freezing, chilly, frosty, wintry
The weather was **cold**.

2. unfriendly, distant, remote
I think she is a **cold** person.

3. virus, flu
I caught a **cold**.

collect

to gather, get together, assemble
We'll **collect** all the glass bottles.

complain

to moan, argue, grumble, object
David wants to **complain** to the waitress.

cool

1. great, excellent, brilliant, fantastic, superb
It was a **cool** movie.

2. chilly
It felt **cool** outside.

copy

1. to duplicate, photocopy, reproduce
I will **copy** the map.

2. fake, counterfeit, forgery
The painting is not the original. It's a **copy**.

correct

1. right, accurate, true, proper
Is this the **correct** meaning?

2. to redo, amend, improve
I had to **correct** my work.

cover

1. to wrap, spread over
Can you **cover** me with the blanket?

2. to hide, conceal, protect, mask
Cover your eyes with these sunglasses.

3. to deal with, handle, contain, include
This CD-ROM **covers** all the topics.

cranky

cross, angry, grumpy
Mom gets very **cranky** if I watch too much TV.

crash

1. noise, bang, clatter
There was a loud **crash** in the kitchen.

2. to topple, fall, tumble, plunge
I watched the rocks **crash** to the beach below.

3. accident, pile-up, collision
There was a bad car **crash** last night.

crazy

wild, frantic, mad, silly
The horse suddenly went **crazy**.

create

to think of, invent, make, design, produce
John will **create** a new chicken recipe.

crowd

group, gang, mass or bunch of people
A **crowd** was watching.

crush

to smash, squash, break, shatter
Don't **crush** the cookies!

cry

1. to weep, sob, wail
Carol started to **cry**.

2. shout, yell, scream
We heard the wolf's **cry**.

cute

sweet, lovable, delightful, charming, nice
He is a **cute** kid.

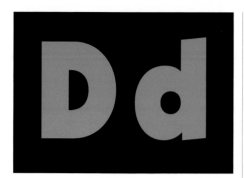

dangerous

1. risky, unsafe, perilous
It is a **dangerous** job.

2. violent, cruel, threatening
He is a **dangerous** criminal.
Opposite: safe

dark

1. gloomy, dingy, shady, shadowy, grim
The room was **dark** and cold.

2. black, starless, pitch-black
The night sky was **dark**.
Opposite: light, bright

decide

to make up your mind, resolve, select, choose
Decide which CD you want.

deep

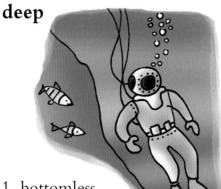

1. bottomless
The diver explored the **deep** sea.

2. low, booming, somber
He had a **deep** voice.

3. rich, intense, dark, vivid
Her eyes were **deep** blue.

delicious

yummy, tasty, scrumptious
This ice cream is **delicious**.

design

to plan, draw, sketch, come up with ideas, create
I will **design** my new car.

different

1. alternative, another, new
I chose a **different** route.

2. mixed, assorted, various
The chocolates were **different** flavors.

3. dissimilar, opposite, opposed
My opinion is **different** from hers.
Opposite: the same, identical

difficult

1. hard, challenging, complicated, tough
The English test was **difficult**.
Opposite: easy

2. uncooperative, annoying, demanding
Lucy is very **difficult** at times.

dirty

grubby, muddy, filthy
His face and hands are **dirty**.

disappoint

to upset, let down, frustrate
I'm sorry to **disappoint** you.

disgusting

horrible, revolting, nasty, foul
The smell from the trash can was **disgusting**.

11

dishonest

insincere, corrupt, lying, untrustworthy, deceitful
He was a **dishonest** man.

disobedient

unruly, rebellious, naughty
Coco is a **disobedient** dog.

draw

1. to sketch, plan, design
I will **draw** a house.

2. attraction, temptation, fascination
The state fair is sure to be a big **draw**.

dry

1. thirsty, parched
My throat is **dry**.
Opposite: wet

2. keen, wicked, fun, wry, sharp
My mom has a **dry** sense of humor.

eager

keen, enthusiastic, excited
Danny was **eager** to play.

earth

1. planet, world
The space shuttle returned to **Earth**.

2. ground, soil, mud, land
Flowers and trees grow in the **earth**.

easy

1. simple, straightforward, uncomplicated
The math test was **easy**.
Opposite: difficult

2. comfortable, undemanding, carefree
Our pet rabbit has an **easy** life.

eat

to have a meal, get some food, dine
Let's **eat** chicken for dinner.
Different ways to **eat**: bite, chew, chomp, munch, nibble, crunch, gobble, swallow

effort

1. hard work, trouble, time, energy
I put a lot of **effort** into this project.

2. attempt, try
Please make an **effort** to score.

empty

1. unfilled, not full
The glass was **empty**.

2. free, vacant, deserted, bare
The house was **empty**.
Opposite: full

end

1. conclusion, finish
Wait until the **end** of the movie.
Opposite: beginning, start, opening

2. back, rear, tail end
We sat at the **end** of the airplane.

3. to stop, finish, cease
We can go out when the thunderstorm **ends**.

enjoy

to like, love, relish, have fun, take pleasure in
I **enjoy** walking the dog.
Opposite: dislike

enormous

huge, gigantic, massive, towering
The new skyscraper was **enormous**.

enough

sufficient, the right amount, plenty
I have eaten **enough**.

excellent

wonderful, marvelous, outstanding, tremendous, first-class, brilliant
The TV program was **excellent**.

exciting

adventurous, thrilling, action-packed, dramatic
The story was really **exciting**.
Opposite: boring

explain

to make clear, describe, tell, spell out
I had to **explain** why I was late.

fade

1. to die away, disappear, dwindle, weaken
Her sadness will **fade** with time.

2. to become dull, bleach out
The color will **fade**.

fair

1. just, honest, unbiased
He is a **fair** person.

2. light, pale, blond
He has **fair** hair.

3. slight, average, reasonable
We had a **fair** chance of getting first prize.

4. festival, carnival
Let's go to the **fair**.

13

fall

1. to **fall** over, tumble, trip, stumble
Be careful you don't **fall**!

2. to drop, go down, decrease
The price might **fall**.
Opposite: rise

false

1. not genuine, untrue, made-up, wrong, incorrect
His facts were **false**.

2. fake, dummy, phoney, artificial
He was wearing a **false** beard.

famous

well-known, leading
He was a **famous** artist.

fantasy

1. made-up, make-believe, fairytale
It was a **fantasy** story.

2. imaginary, dream, unreal
You live in a **fantasy** world!

fast

1. quick, speedy
Dad has a **fast** car.

2. quickly, speedily, rapidly, at a great pace
I work **fast**.

fat

1. chubby, plump, pudgy, overweight
George is a bit **fat**.

2. thick, heavy, huge, bulky
It is a **fat** book.

favorite

special, most-loved, most wanted
Is this your **favorite** kitten?

feeling

1. emotion, mood, affection, warmth
John found it hard to show his **feelings**.

2. sensation, intuition, instinct, suspicion
I have the **feeling** we are being watched.

fight

1. to wrestle, tussle, grapple
The boys started to **fight**.

2. Types of **fights**: battle, war, brawl, contest, boxing match, argument

fill

to put into, pour into, load
First **fill** the pot with soil.

find

1. to hunt, root out, discover, track down
The officer will **find** the burglar.

2. to come across, locate, uncover
I can **find** that book at the library.

fine

1. bright, good, pleasant
The weather is **fine**.

2. penalty, ticket
I got a **fine** for speeding.

3. delicate, dainty, light, fragile
The embroidery is very **fine**.

4. excellent, great, tremendous, wonderful
He wrote a **fine** essay.

5. thin, slight
He drew a **fine** line.

finish

1. to end, conclude, complete, stop
He will **finish** his speech later.

2. to eat up, consume, polish off
Did you **finish** my chocolate?

fix

1. to mend, repair
The mechanic will **fix** the car.

2. scrape, trouble
I got myself into a **fix**.

flat

1. even, smooth, level, horizontal
Put the balls on a **flat** surface.

2. punctured, burst, blown out
He has a **flat** tire.

float

1. to drift, flutter, glide
The balloon **floats** in the sky.

2. to stay up, remain on the surface
The rubber duck will **float**.

floppy

droopy, loose, sagging
My rabbit has **floppy** ears.

flow

1. to run, stream, gush, pour
The river **flows** quickly.

2. flood, rush, stream
The **flow** of articles on the subject is amazing.

fly

1. to hover, glide, float, soar, swoop
Look how high the eagle can **fly**.

2. to dash, rush, race off, hurry
I can't stay, I've got to **fly**.

3. to operate an airplane, take control, pilot
He was **flying** by himself.

foggy

misty, gloomy, hazy, cloudy
It was a **foggy** day.

follow

1. to walk behind, tail, go after, chase, pursue
The kids started to **follow** me.

2. to understand, get, grasp
I don't **follow** this game.

3. to go along, take, travel along
Follow this road and then take a right.

free

1. no cost, no charge
It's **free** to get in.

2. to release, liberate
I will **free** him from his chores.

3. empty, not occupied, vacant, available
The parking space was **free**.

freeze

1. to ice over, harden, go solid
The pond will **freeze**.

2. go numb, get cold
You'll **freeze** outside!

fresh

1. new, clean
I'll change into some **fresh** clothes.

2. original, inventive, different
We need to get some **fresh** ideas.

3. natural, raw, unprocessed
Fresh food is good for you.

friendly

sociable, affectionate, warm, loving, welcoming
The neighbors are very **friendly**.
Opposite: unfriendly

frightening

scary, creepy, spooky, horrifying, terrifying
The story was **frightening**.

full

1. crammed, overloaded, brimming, packed
The suitcase was **full**.

2. satisfied, stuffed, well-fed
I'm **full** now.

3. complete, thorough, entire
Let's hear the **full** story.

funny

1. amusing, comic, humorous, witty, hilarious
He told me a **funny** joke.

2. strange, odd, peculiar, bizarre
The cheese has a **funny** taste.

game

sport, pastime, hobby, recreation, entertainment
Baseball is a popular **game** in the U.S.

generous

1. giving, kind, unselfish
Mr. Williams is very **generous** with his money.

2. large, big, oversized
That's a **generous** portion of chocolate cake.

gentle

1. soft, delicate, careful, tender
She was very **gentle** with the baby.

2. light, slight, pleasant, faint, mild
A **gentle** breeze blew.

get

1. to fetch, bring, take hold of, retrieve
Go and **get** the ball.

2. to buy, find, obtain
Where did you **get** that kite?

3. to become, grow, turn
I will **get** hot in this hat.

4. to persuade, convince, coax, make
I'll **get** him to come, too.

give

1. to pass, hand
Could you **give** me the dessert?

2. to communicate, tell, offer, present
I will **give** him the information.

3. to donate, contribute
My family **gives** money to cancer research.

glad

happy, pleased, content
Billy was **glad** to see his friend.

good

1. welcome, great, splendid, superb
That's **good** news.

2. talented, capable, accomplished, skilled
She's a **good** golfer.

3. decent, kind, trustworthy, honest
They are **good** people.
Opposite: bad

great

1. excellent, marvelous, fantastic, fabulous
The day trip was **great**.

2. grand, magnificent, splendid, luxurious
Great red roses filled their garden.

3. huge, long, immense
It was a **great** distance to travel.

4. intense, considerable, acute
It was a time of **great** sadness to me.

gross

awful, dreadful, terrible, bad, disgusting
That meal was really **gross**.

group

1. to gather, assemble, collect
Group everyone together.

2. club, association, band, society, gang
Please come and join our **group**.

3. **Groups** of animals: herd, flock of birds/sheep, school of dolphins/whales, gaggle of geese, litter of kittens/puppies, pack of hounds/wolves, pride of lions

grow

1. to increase in height, get bigger, get taller
Will my plant **grow**?

2. to increase, develop, expand
Support for our new club will **grow**.

3. to develop, sprout, germinate
He wants to **grow** flowers.

4. to start, get to, come to
Do you think Hannah will **grow** to like broccoli?

hang

1. to grasp, keep hold of, cling to
Hang on to the cliff.

2. to drop down, be suspended
Icicles **hang** from the doorway.

3. to put up, nail, stick
Let's **hang** the picture here.

happy

pleased, delighted, glad, cheerful, content, joyful
Grace was so **happy** to see her friends again.

Opposite: sad

hard

1. difficult, complex, complicated
I thought the questions were **hard**.

2. solid, firm, stony
The ground was **hard**.

3. tiring, exhausting, tough
It was **hard** work.

hate

to dislike, loathe, cannot stand, detest
I **hate** cabbage.

Opposite: like

heavy

1. overweight, plump, stout, chubby
He looks a bit **heavy**.

2. weighty, cumbersome
Her big suitcase was very **heavy**.

3. thick, dense, nonstop
Heavy snow was forecast the next day.

Opposite: light

help

1. to be of assistance, aid, give support to
Police officers **help** motorists.

2. support, assistance, guidance, backing
The man needed **help**.

hide

to conceal, put away, cover up
Let's **hide** the book here.

high

1. tall, towering, lofty
We walked up the **high** mountain.

2. excellent, outstanding, exceptional, top-class
We expect a **high** standard of work from you.

3. expensive, excessive, over the top, overinflated
We can't afford the **high** prices.

hit

Ways to **hit**: to poke, prod, jab, thump, bump, knock, bang, bash, beat, strike, smash, punch

honest

sincere, truthful, trustworthy, genuine, honorable
He is an **honest** person.
Opposite: dishonest

horrible

1. disgusting, revolting, nasty, foul, dreadful, horrid
The meal was **horrible**.

2. terrifying, frightening, vile, hideous
The prince came face to face with a **horrible** monster.

hot

1. sticky, warm, humid
It was such a **hot** day.

2. roaring, blazing, glowing, scorching
We sat in front of the **hot** fire.

3. spicy, peppery
This chili is very **hot**.

hungry

ravenous, famished, starving
The cat felt **hungry**.

hurry

to rush, zoom, dash, race, run
Hurry to the store.

hurt

1. to harm, injure, abuse
He wouldn't **hurt** that dog.

2. to damage, ruin, spoil
Looking at the sun will **hurt** your eyes.

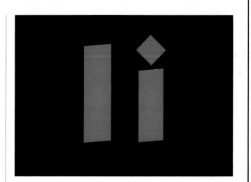

icy

1. slippery, frozen, dangerous
The lake is **icy**.

2. hard, cold, frosty, chilly
Mom gave me an **icy** look.

idea

thought, suggestion, brainstorm
It was my **idea**.

important

1. crucial, essential, vital, necessary
It's an **important** document.

2. famous, well-known, powerful
He is an **important** politician.

interesting

intriguing, fascinating, spellbinding, exciting, gripping
This story is quite **interesting**.

Opposite: dull

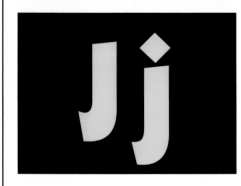

journey

Types of **journeys**: flight, voyage, cruise, drive, expedition, safari, trip, tour

jump

1. to leap, hop, spring, bound
Jump over the hole.

2. to start, flinch, wince
You made me **jump**.

3. rise, increase, hike
There has been a big **jump** in the price.

junk

rubbish, mess, clutter, trash, garbage, litter
There is so much **junk** in your room.

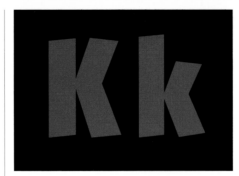

keep

1. to store, hold, look after, put away
Are you sure you want to **keep** this bug?

2. to carry on, continue, persevere, stick with
Keep going!

3. to feed, look after, support
It costs a lot to **keep** a pony.

kind

1. generous, well-meaning, nice, thoughtful, considerate
Giving away your prize money was very **kind**.

2. type, species, sort, breed
What **kind** of dog do you have?

3. brand, make, sort
What **kind** of sneakers do you wear?

knock

1. to bang, pound, tap, rap
I will **knock** on the door.

2. to hit, thump, bash, bump
I **knock** into things all the time.

know

1. to recognize, remember
I **know** that woman.

2. to understand, have knowledge of, be familiar with
I **know** how to speak Spanish.

3. to be sure, be certain
I don't **know** if he saw me.

knowledge

1. information, facts, wisdom
Books are a great source of **knowledge**.

2. understanding, awareness, expertise in
He has a great **knowledge** of boats.

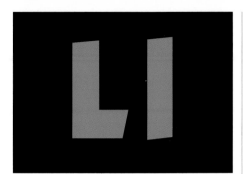

land

1. to touch down, arrive, dock
The helicopter will **land** at one o'clock.

2. soil, earth, fields
The farmer plowed the **land**.

3. estate, property, grounds
How big is his **land**?

4. country, nation
Australia is a **land** far from here.

last

1. final, concluding
He raced to catch the **last** bus home.

2. to go on, continue
How long does this movie **last**?

late

overdue, delayed
The bus is **late**.

laugh

to chuckle, giggle, snicker
He never **laughs** at my jokes.

lazy

idle, inactive, slothful
My **lazy** uncle watches TV all day.

learn

to find out, discover, study, practice, master
Jim wants to **learn** how to swim.

leave

1. to depart, go, set off
The train **leaves** at 5 o'clock.

2. holiday, vacation, time off
How much **leave** do you have?

lie

1. to tell an untruth, mislead, fib
Did you **lie** to your brother?

2. lay down, sprawl out
I want to **lie** on my bed.

light

1. to set on fire, set alight, ignite
Wait until I **light** the fire.

2. not heavy, flimsy, underweight
The bag was so **light**.

3. glow, glimmer, gleam, beam, illumination
Heidi saw a **light** in the distance.

4. airy, bright, sunny, well-lit
The room was **light**.

like

1. to be fond of, respect, admire
I **like** all my friends.

2. the same, identical, similar to
My coat is just **like** yours.

3. to want, desire, prefer
Which flavor would you **like**?

little
small, tiny, petite, miniature, minute
The newborn kitten was **little**.

lively
energetic, enthusiastic, active, full of life
Danny is very **lively**.

long

1. lengthy, endless
The snake is **long**.
Opposite: short

2. to yearn, desire, want, wish
Emma **longed** to go to the beach.

look

1. to gaze at, view, study, stare
Look at the wonderful view.

2. to search, hunt, track down
Michael helped me **look** for my bag.

3. to seem, come across as, appear
The man **looks** a bit threatening.

lost

1. missing, vanished, gone
My pet rabbit is **lost**.
Opposite: found

2. bewildered, confused, unsure, disoriented
You're looking a bit **lost**.

3. missed, wasted
Al wished he had gone to college. It was a **lost** opportunity.

loud
1. noisy, deafening, raucous
The music was far too **loud**.
Opposite: quiet

2. gaudy, over-the-top, flashy
His shirt was very **loud**.

love

1. to cherish, adore, worship
I **love** her so much.
Opposite: hate

2. to like, enjoy, be fond of
I **love** going to the movies.

3. passion, yearning, regard, devotion to
Sailors have a great **love** of the sea.

low
1. bad, poor, unsatisfactory
I have a **low** opinion of cheaters.

2. short, little, small, squat
The horse jumped over a **low** fence.
Opposite: high

3. unhappy, miserable, sad
My brother is feeling **low**.

4. quiet, hushed, soft
Her voice was **low**.

mad

1. angry, furious, livid
My sister was **mad** that I had borrowed her jeans.

2. insane, a lunatic, mentally ill
People thought that the old man was **mad**.

main

major, primary, most important, chief, vital
The **main** reason for coming is to tell you about the trip.

make

1. to put together, produce, construct, build, create
He will **make** a tent from some old sheets.

2. to come up with, invent, devise, think up

I am sure he can **make** a machine to do it!

3. to force, compel, order
The teacher will **make** the bully stay for detention.

4. to fix, arrange, book
I'll **make** another appointment for you.

make-believe

imaginary, dreamt-up, invented, made-up
It was a **make-believe** story.
Opposite: real

many

a lot of, a great deal of, thousands, numerous, heaps of
The goose has **many** goslings.

mean

1. cruel, harsh, horrible, heartless, nasty, rotten
It was a **mean** trick to play on him.

2. to intend, plan, aim, propose
I **mean** to do this walk.

3. to stand for, represent, translate as
What does this German word **mean**?

23

meet
1. to come together, join, run into, merge with
The stream **meets** the river near our town.

2. to see, join up with
I'll **meet** you outside the park.

3. to assemble, congregate, join together
All the teams will **meet** in the stadium.

messy
1. disorganized, cluttered, untidy, chaotic, a shambles
Your room is too **messy**.

2. scruffy, crumpled, disheveled
Greg looks so **messy**.

mix
1. to scramble, combine, muddle, jumble
Don't **mix** up the cards.

2. to stir together, blend
Mix the flour and the eggs.

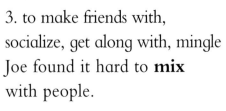

3. to make friends with, socialize, get along with, mingle
Joe found it hard to **mix** with people.

modern
up-to-date, trendy, stylish fashionable
The new café is great. It's so **modern**.
Opposite: old-fashioned

monster
1. horror, terror, nuisance, pain
The twins are little **monsters**.

2. Types of **monster**: dragon, beast, giant, hobgoblin, vampire, werewolf, troll.
The **monster** groaned.

more
extra, added, additional, new
There will be **more** space when we clear out the garage.

move
1. to relocate, change address
I'm looking forward to the day we **move**.

2. to shift, budge, push
Don't **move** the chairs.

3. to creep, tip-toe
Move slowly toward the injured bird.

near
close to, not far from, beside
We were **near** home.
Opposite: far

neat
1. tidy, orderly, organized
There was a **neat** row of desks.

2. cute, good, cool, likeable
He was a **neat** guy.

nervous
anxious, scared, frightened, twitchy, jumpy
Louise felt **nervous** about going on the flight.

never

not ever, definitely not, absolutely not, at no time
I will **never** do it again.

new

1. fresh, original, inventive
She took a **new** approach to the problem.

2. modern, recent, up-to-date
Our house is quite **new**.
Opposite: old

nice

1. lovely, beautiful, fine, pleasant
What a **nice** day!

2. cheerful, friendly, kind, considerate
Georgia is a **nice** girl.

night

dark, night-time, darkness, evening, after dark
The city looks pretty at **night**.

noise

1. racket, uproar, commotion
Don't make so much **noise**!

2. sound
We couldn't hear any **noise**.

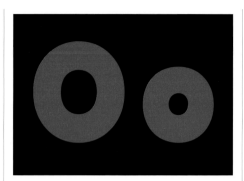

off

1. cancelled, postponed
The school trip is **off**.

2. not in use, not on, not operating
The lights are **off**.

often

frequently, regularly, constantly, again and again
I **often** walk to school with my sister.

old

1. ancient, run-down, falling apart
The bridge is **old** and creaky.

2. elderly, aged
My grandfather is very **old**.

3. worn-out, shabby, scruffy, tattered
My sneakers are **old**.

open

1. to undo, unfasten, release, unlock
Could you **open** the door?

2. unwrap
I can't wait to **open** my present.

3. wide-open, clear, deserted, empty
It's **open** country from here.

pain

1. agony, torture, hurt
I'm in **pain**.

2. ache, twinge, pang, cramp
I felt a **pain** in my mouth.

part

1. area, district, neighborhood
In which **part** of the city do you live?

2. to give away, hand over, donate
Tommy didn't want to **part** with any money.

3. role, character, leading role
I'm playing the **part** of Dorothy.

4. piece, portion, bit, percentage
He wanted his **part** of the fortune.

pass

1. to hand, give
Could you **pass** me the ball?

2. to drive past, go past, move along
I'm waiting for the bus to **pass**.

3. to succeed, get through
My big brother must **pass** his driving test.

4. to go away, fade, disappear, vanish
The pain of the injection will soon **pass**.

pay

1. to spend, give, hand over
You have to **pay** $10 for the book.

2. to answer for, be punished for, regret
He said, "You'll **pay** for this!"

peace

1. quietness, quiet, calmness, tranquility
I went into my room alone to get some **peace**.

2. harmony, goodwill, understanding, reconciliation
The organization hopes that **peace** will come to the world.

perfect

1. ideal, wonderful, excellent
It was a **perfect** start to the day.

2. immaculate, flawless, faultless
The house was in **perfect** condition.

pick

1. to choose, select, go for, opt for
Jenny didn't know which pet to **pick**.

2. to gather, collect
We went to **pick** strawberries.

piece

1. portion, slice, helping, bit, chunk
Could I have a **piece** of cake?

2. fragment, splinter, shard
Be careful you don't cut yourself on a **piece** of glass.

pile

1. heap, mound, stack
Throw it on the **pile** of garbage.

2. to stack, put
Please **pile** them over there.

place

1. town, city, area, district, neighborhood
Where is your favorite **place** to live?

2. spot, position, location, site
Mark the **place** with an X.

3. to put, leave, lay
Place the plates here.

play

1. to have fun, entertain yourselves, mess around
Go and **play** in the park.

2. to compete against, challenge, take on
Our team will **play** yours on Saturday.

3. drama, performance, show
The **play** has five acts.

pleased

thrilled, overjoyed, happy, delighted, glad
I am so **pleased** you got a place.

plenty

lots of, enough, heaps of, a great deal of
We have **plenty** of food for the party.

polite

courteous, well-mannered, considerate
The manager was very **polite**.

poor

1. penniless, needy
The families are **poor**.

2. mediocre, inadequate, dismal, weak, feeble
I was angry at the **poor** response.

3. unfortunate, unlucky
The **poor** girl was soaked to the skin.

power

1. influence, importance, clout
The Senators have a lot of **power**.

2. right, authority, say-so, ability
I have the **power** to stop the game.

3. force, energy, strength, might
Lightning has the **power** to split a tree.

pretty

1. cute, good-looking, attractive, beautiful
Her granddaughter is very **pretty**.

2. picturesque, charming, quaint
The cottages are very **pretty**.

proud

1. haughty, arrogant, snobbish, conceited
She is a **proud** woman.

2. pleased with, happy for, delighted for
I was so **proud** of the team.

pull

1. to tug, yank
Pull the cord.

2. to tow
The car will **pull** the horse trailer.

3. to drag, heave, haul
Pull the skis up the hill.

push

1. to shove, force, thrust, press
He tried to **push** me into the wall.

2. to nudge open, press open
Push the door.

put

1. to place, lay, leave, set
Put the books on the table.

2. to stick, poke, dip, jab
He **put** his finger in the peanut butter.

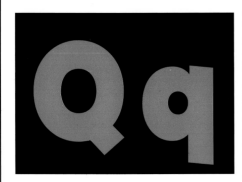

quick

1. fast, speedy, swift
He's a **quick** runner.
Opposite: slow

2. instant, immediate, rapid
Dad needs a **quick** answer.

3. bright, efficient, clever
She's a **quick** learner.

quiet

1. silent
Be **quiet**!

2. soft, hushed, low
The teacher had a **quiet** voice.

3. reserved, withdrawn, shy, timid
He is a **quiet** boy.

quite

1. completely, absolutely, definitely, totally
We are **quite** sure we saw him.

2. pretty, fairly, reasonably
We are **quite** close now.

race

1. to run, rush, hurry, dash
Carol had to **race** to the mailbox.

2. to compete, challenge, run
I will **race** in the state track meet.

rain

1. to pour, drizzle
It is going to **rain**.

2. Types of **rain**: **rain**drops, shower, drizzle, downpour, torrential **rain**

reach

1. to come to, arrive at, get to, travel to
How long will it take us to **reach** the shore?

2. to touch, get to, stretch up to
Gary couldn't **reach** the top shelf.

ready

1. prepared, all set
Are you **ready** to go out?

2. handy, available
Have you got your money for the bus **ready**?

real

1. genuine, authentic
The little pine tree was **real**.

2. true, sincere, good, honest
John has been a **real** friend.

rest

1. nap, sleep, snooze, doze
My brother needed a **rest** after playing soccer.

2. remainder
I'll walk the **rest** of the way.

3. to sleep, take a break, slow down, relax, lie down
I need to **rest**.

4. to stand, prop, lean, put
Rest the broom against the wall.

return

1. to come back, come home
The bus **returns** at ten o'clock.

2. to take back, swap, get a refund
I will **return** the top because it doesn't fit.

rich

1. well-off, prosperous, wealthy
He was a very **rich** man.

2. deep, vivid, luscious
The paint was a lovely **rich** red.

ride

Things you can **ride** on/**ride** in: horse, bicycle, motorcycle, automobile, truck, airplane, bus, train

right

1. correct
I knew I was **right**.
Opposite: wrong

2. I am **right**-handed.
Opposite: left

3. fair, proper, honest, honorable
It was **right** to tell the truth.

roll

1. to push, whirl, spin
Roll the ball to the baby.

2. tube, reel
Mom needs another **roll** of paper.

3. to press down, flatten, level
Roll out the dough on the table.

rough

1. choppy, stormy, unsettled, wild
The sea is **rough** today.

2. outline, sketchy, basic, simple
Do a **rough** drawing first.

3. coarse, scratchy, bristly, itchy
My dad's beard feels **rough**.

4. approximate, vague
It's a **rough** guess, but I think there are about 50 in the box.

5. tough, violent, harsh
I think boxing is quite a **rough** sport.

round

Round shapes: ball, circle, coin, pizza, CD-ROM, plate, orange

rude

impolite, misbehaved, impudent, disrespectful
What a **rude** man!

sad

1. miserable, unhappy, downcast, tearful, heartbroken
I was **sad** when we left our old house.

2. depressing, tragic, upsetting, heartbreaking
The teacher had some **sad** news.

3. moving, touching, heartrending
The end of the story is very **sad**.

safe

1. secure, out of danger, protected
Inside the house we were **safe** from the storm.

2. careful, attentive, observant, sensible
My dad is a **safe** driver.

3. harmless, tame, docile
Don't worry; the reef sharks are **safe**.

save

1. to rescue, free, liberate, release
We tried to **save** the trapped swans.

2. to keep, collect, hold on to
I will **save** these stamps for my collection.

say

1. to reply, answer, exclaim
Harry **says** that we can go fishing later today.

2. to state, relate, pronounce, suggest
What does the first page **say**?

3. to tell, talk about, reveal, communicate, express
Sally won't **say** what's wrong.

scare

to frighten, shock, alarm, terrify
Luke was afraid he might **scare** his friend.

search

1. to look, look high and low, hunt, explore
We may have to **search** for hours.

2. hunt, exploration, close look
The police launched a huge **search**.

secret

1. private, confidential
I'm not telling you; it's **secret** information.

2. hidden, concealed, disguised
They looked for the **secret** tunnel.

see

1. to find out, discover
I'll **see** if I can find him for you.

2. to catch a glimpse of, glimpse, catch sight of, spot, make out
I can **see** the train in the distance.

3. to meet, have a word with, talk to, speak to
The teacher wants to **see** me after school.

send

1. to mail, post
I'll **send** you the letter.

2. to fax, e-mail, forward
I will **send** her a message.

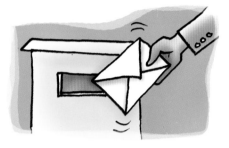

separate

1. another, different, alternative
I'll send the ticket in a **separate** envelope.

2. to split up, break up, divide, fragment
Make sure the group doesn't **separate**.

3. to divorce, split up, live apart
My parents are going to **separate**.

set

1. to solidify, harden, thicken
My aunt waited for the jam to **set**.

2. to take place, locate, happen
The story is **set** in a magical world.

3. fixed, arranged, regular, established
Lessons start at **set** times.

shadow

silhouette, figure, shape
I made a rabbit **shadow** on the wall.

shake

1. to quiver, quake, tremble
He started to **shake** with fear.

2. to shudder, vibrate
The building started to **shake** as the train went past.

shape

1. to form, make, mold
Shape your dough into a loaf.

2. Types of **shapes**: circle, square, rectangle, triangle, oval, diamond, star, hexagon

3. outline, form, look
The **shape** of this house is quite different.

share

1. to divide, distribute, split
Share the cookies with your sister.

2. portion, part, percentage, bit
He got his **share** of the prize money.

sharp

1. shooting, stabbing, piercing
Mark felt a **sharp** pain in his side.

2. razor-sharp, pointed

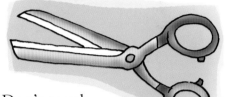

Don't touch those **sharp** scissors.

3. intelligent, wise, on the ball, smart
Mike is a **sharp** student.

shiny

polished, gleaming, glossy
I wore my **shiny** new shoes.

short

1. small, little, tiny, petite
My sister is tall, but I am **short**.

2. to be lacking, be without
I'm **short** on cash.

3. brief, concise
I'd like to read you a **short** poem.

Opposites: tall, long

shout

to yell, shriek, call, scream, cry out
He was so angry, he started to **shout** at me.

show

1. to present, let me see, reveal
Will you **show** me your picture?

2. to represent, illustrate, portray, feature
What does this painting **show**?

3. to demonstrate, explain, describe, tell
I'll **show** you how to make a model of a stegosaurus.

4. play, musical, exhibition
I can't wait to go to the **show**.

shy

timid, nervous, modest, bashful
He's a bit **shy**.

side

1. team, group
Which **side** do you want to play on?

2. edge, perimeter
Go to the **side** of the swimming pool.

3. face, surface
Write your name on this **side** of the box.

sign

1. notice, poster, signpost
The **sign** said we should go this way.

2. to write your name
Sign at the bottom.

3. signal, warning, indication
Lightning is a **sign** of a thunderstorm.

silly

foolish, stupid, ridiculous, goofy
Don't be **silly**!

sleepy

tired, exhausted, drowsy
Meg felt **sleepy** after watching TV.

slip

1. to fall, tumble, slide, skid
I could **slip** on the ice.

2. piece of paper, strip
Write your name on this **slip**.

slow

1. steady, unhurried, long, drawn out
The snail's pace is **slow**.

2. running behind time
My alarm clock is **slow**.
Opposite: fast

3. slow-moving, boring, dull, uneventful
The story is **slow**.

small

1. little, tiny, minute
The fish was so **small**.

2. minor, modest, slight
If I can help in a **small** way, I will.

smart

1. clever, intelligent, bright, wise
Lyle is a **smart** student.

2. well dressed, stylish, neat, tidy
John looked very **smart** in his new suit.

3. clever, flippant, sarcastic
I'm tired of your **smart** comments.

smell

1. aroma, scent, fragrance, perfume
The flowers have a lovely **smell**.

2. to sniff, detect
I can **smell** bacon.

3. stench, stink, odor
What a dreadful **smell**!

smooth

1. silky, soft, velvety
The baby's skin is so **smooth**.

2. calm, gentle, uneventful, tranquil
I hope the ferry crossing will be **smooth**.

3. even, delicate, graceful, light
Make **smooth** strokes with your paintbrush.

sneaky

sly, cunning, devious
That was a **sneaky** trick to play.

soft

1. hushed, gentle, quiet, low
Her voice was **soft**.

2. feathery, spongy, springy
I like **soft** pillows.

3. fluffy, smooth, silky
The chick's feathers are so **soft**.

space

1. room
Is there any **space** for my toys?

2. the universe, solar system, galaxy, outer space
The astronauts flew into **space**.

3. gap, hole, opening
Let's fill the **space** with sand.

speak

to talk, communicate, express yourself
Dad **speaks** in a loud voice.

speed

1. pace, rate
He can type at such a great **speed**.

2. to go too fast, go over the limit, drive too fast
Don't **speed**!

3. to zoom, race, hurtle, fly
I can **speed** down the hill on my bike.

start

1. to begin, commence, get going
We have to **start** the race on time.

2. to introduce, create, initiate
My brother is going to **start** a book club.

3. the beginning, first moments, opening
I hate missing the **start** of a movie.

stay

1. to remain, stop, wait, linger
I told my dog to **stay**; I'll be right back.

2. to come to, visit, sleep at, stop over
Would you like to **stay** at our house?

3. to keep on, walk on, continue, remain
The park keeper told us to **stay** on the path.

stick

1. to glue, paste, join
Stick the two pieces of paper together.

2. to jab, prod, put, poke, dip
Don't **stick** your finger in the frosting!

3. twig, branch
He threw a **stick** for the puppy to fetch.

4. to stay with, continue, not give up, persevere
He decided to **stick** with homework instead of playing outside.

stop

1. to cease, refrain from, finish, quit
Stop talking!

2. to come to a halt, come to a stop, come to a standstill
The crossing guard told the cars to **stop**.

3. to stay, take a break, visit
We are going to **stop** in New York before going to Boston.

strong

1. tough, fit, hefty, muscular
He is **strong** because he lifts weights.
Opposite: weak

2. forceful, powerful, iron
Ali has a **strong** will.

3. overpowering, intense, fierce
There's a **strong** smell of paint.

sure

certain, definite, convinced, positive
I'm **sure** I left my hat here.

surprise

to shock, amaze, stun, startle
I was **surprised** that she had won the competition.

sweet

1. nice, kind-hearted, generous, pleasant
Your friend is so **sweet**.

2. sugary, syrupy
It tastes too **sweet**.
Opposite: sour

take

1. to bring, carry, move
I'll **take** the chairs inside.

2. to need, require, demand
It will **take** weeks of cleaning to shine again.

3. to steal, pinch, seize
Did they **take** the jewels?

talk

1. to discuss, chat, chatter
We will **talk** about our hobbies.

2. conversation, chat, discussion
I'd like to have a **talk** with the zoo keeper.

3. speech, presentation
Our **talk** today is about recycling.

tall

towering, high, gigantic
The **tall** towers of the castle loomed over us.
Opposite: short

taste

1. to try, sample, eat, have
Would you like to **taste** the apple pie?

2. flavor
I love the **taste** of toffee ice cream.
The way things **taste**: hot, bitter, sweet, sour, spicy, fruity, creamy, salty, bland, stale, fresh

tear

to rip, split, slash, cut, slit
Mom warned me not to **tear** my new T-shirt.

terrible

dreadful, awful, bad, horrible
It was a **terrible** mistake.

thick

1. creamy, smooth
Stir the sauce until it is **thick**.

2. dense, overgrown, heavy, lush
We bicycled through a **thick** forest.

3. wide, broad, solid
The walls of the old cottage are really **thick**.

thin

1. skinny, underweight, slim, slender, bony
He looks too **thin**.

2. see-through, flimsy, lightweight, fine
The material is too **thin**.

think

1. to ponder, consider, concentrate, reflect
Leave me alone;
I need to **think**.

2. to believe, feel, be sure, be convinced
We **think** he is the best person for the job.

3. to imagine, assume, suppose, guess
I **think** it's nearly six o'clock.

thoughtful

considerate, kind, helpful, understanding
That is very **thoughtful** of you.

throw

to pass, fling, hurl, toss
Throw the ball to me.

tired

1. exhausted, weary, sleepy, worn out, drowsy
It's late and I'm **tired**.

2. to be fed up with, have enough of, be sick of, be bored with
Vicky is **tired** of getting up early every day.

top

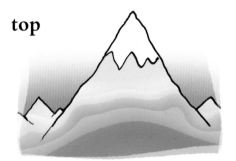

1. peak, summit, highest point
We will climb to the **top** of the mountain.

2. lid, cap, stopper
Put the **top** back on the bottle.

3. highest scoring, best, leading
Rex was the **top** dog in his group.

touch

to feel, handle, finger, hold, pick up
Don't **touch** the ornaments.

trash

rubbish, garbage, junk, refuse
I'll take the **trash** to the dump.

treat

1. surprise, special occasion, present
Going to the theme park was a **treat**.

2. to look after, behave toward, act toward
How did they **treat** the prisoners?

3. to look after, give treatment to, care for
Is the doctor going to **treat** you?

trouble

bother, worry, anxiety
My brother causes so much **trouble**.

true

1. correct, right, accurate
Is it **true** that you're going to another school?
Opposite: false

2. loyal, devoted, genuine, real, faithful, trustworthy
Maisie is a **true** friend.

try

1. to strive, aim, attempt, make an effort
I must **try** to do my homework.

2. to sample, taste, nibble
May I **try** the chicken?

turn

1. go, chance, opportunity
It's my **turn** to sing next.

2. to spin, whirl, twirl, revolve
I could see the sails of the windmill start to **turn** in the breeze.

3. to change, convert, make, transform
My parents will **turn** the room into a nursery.

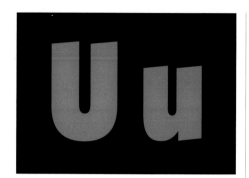

ugly

unattractive, disgusting, repulsive, hideous
Jack stood in front of the **ugly** beast.

uncomfortable

1. painful, tight
This belt is **uncomfortable**.

2. embarrassed, self-conscious, awkward, uneasy
She makes me feel **uncomfortable**.

understand

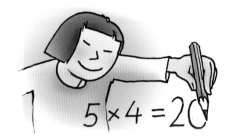

to know, realize, grasp, follow, see
I **understand** multiplication now.

upset

1. distressed, sad, tearful, hurt
I could see she was **upset**.

2. to worry, bother, distress, alarm, hurt
The news might **upset** her.

useful

1. helpful, valuable, a good idea
Learning a language is always **useful**.

2. practical, handy, an advantage, worthwhile
It's **useful** to have a computer.

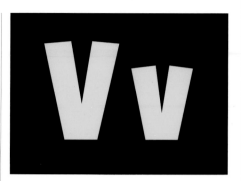

vacation

holiday, break
We're going to Florida for our **vacation**.

very

extremely, really, so, tremendously
I am **very** pleased you came.

visit

1. to drop in on, go to, take a trip to
Our class is going to **visit** the museum.

2. to stay with, stay over
I promise I'll **visit** you at Christmas.

vote

to choose, select, pick, elect, select
Who did you **vote** for?

wait

1. to stay, remain, stay put
Wait outside.

2. to delay, hesitate, hang on
I can't **wait** any longer.

walk

1. to go on foot, stroll, amble
Let's **walk** to the library.

2. to tread, trample, step, walk over
Don't **walk** on the grass.
Ways to **walk**: to stride, march, plod, saunter, wander, sneak, trudge

want

to wish for, desire, long for, yearn for
Tom **wants** a bicycle for his birthday.

warm

1. pleasant, sultry, humid, mild, balmy
It was a **warm** evening.

2. cozy, snug
I'm **warm** in this jacket.

3. tepid, lukewarm
The water is **warm**, not hot.

wash

to clean, scrub, polish, shampoo
I **wash** my hair in the sink.

waste

1. to fritter away, throw away, not use, squander
I hate to **waste** the rest of this paper.

2. rubbish, scrap, junk, trash, garbage, litter, refuse
I'll throw the **waste** in the bin.

watch

1. to look at, gaze at, study, observe
I can **watch** the birds on the lake.

2. to be aware of, be alert to, pay attention to
We must **watch** for any sign of danger.

weak

1. feeble, frail
He was exhausted and **weak**.
Opposite: strong

2. tired, fragile, delicate, faint
I felt so **weak** after the flu.

3. indecisive, timid, cowardly, pathetic
He is a **weak** person.

weird

strange, bizarre, odd, peculiar
What a **weird** creature!

well

better, strong, fit, healthy, good
I feel **well** again.
Opposite: ill

wet

1. drenched, sodden, soaked
He got **wet** in the rain.

2. rainy, drizzly, showery, pouring rain
If it's **wet**, we're not allowed to go out.

wild

1. crazy, zany
That's a **wild** idea!

2. the natural environment, natural surroundings, bush, plain, open air
Monkeys live in the **wild**.

3. rowdy, loud, boisterous, disruptive
Such **wild** behavior won't be tolerated.

wonder

1. to think about, ask yourself, puzzle over
I **wonder** why the stars are so bright.

2. in amazement, open-mouthed, in awe, in surprise
The ballerina looked at the stage in **wonder**.

wonderful

marvelous, fabulous, brilliant, terrific, superb
It is **wonderful** to see you.

work

1. to be employed, do a job, earn a living

My uncle **works** as a builder.

2. to get going, operate, use
I can't **work** the camera.

world

1. the planet, Earth
I'd like to travel around the **world**.

2. universe
There is a **world** of things to learn in the encyclopedia.

worry

1. to be anxious, be concerned, fret, get agitated
Don't **worry**; I'll be fine.

2. distress, anxiety, concern, unease
That dog causes us a lot of **worry**.

wrong

1. incorrect, false, untrue, inaccurate
The answer is **wrong**.
Opposite: right

2. immoral, dishonest, illegal, wicked
It's **wrong** to steal.

X-ray
photograph, picture
The doctor took an **X-ray** of Joe's ankle.

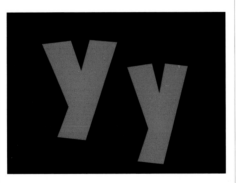

yell
to shout, scream, holler
Don't **yell** at me.

young
1. babyish, childish, silly immature, infantile
Josh is **young** for his age.

2. babies, litter, offspring
The leopard protected her **young**.

3. small, preschool, little
I teach **young** children.

zero
nothing, nil, zip
Our team scored **zero**.

zigzag

jagged, crooked, bendy, wiggly
Draw a **zigzag** pattern across the page.

zoo
wildlife park, animal park, safari park
We're going to the **zoo**.

zoom
to hurtle, speed, rush
We watched the rocket **zoom** into the sky.